Mandala Coloring Book

Refresh the Brain

Andrea T. Cross

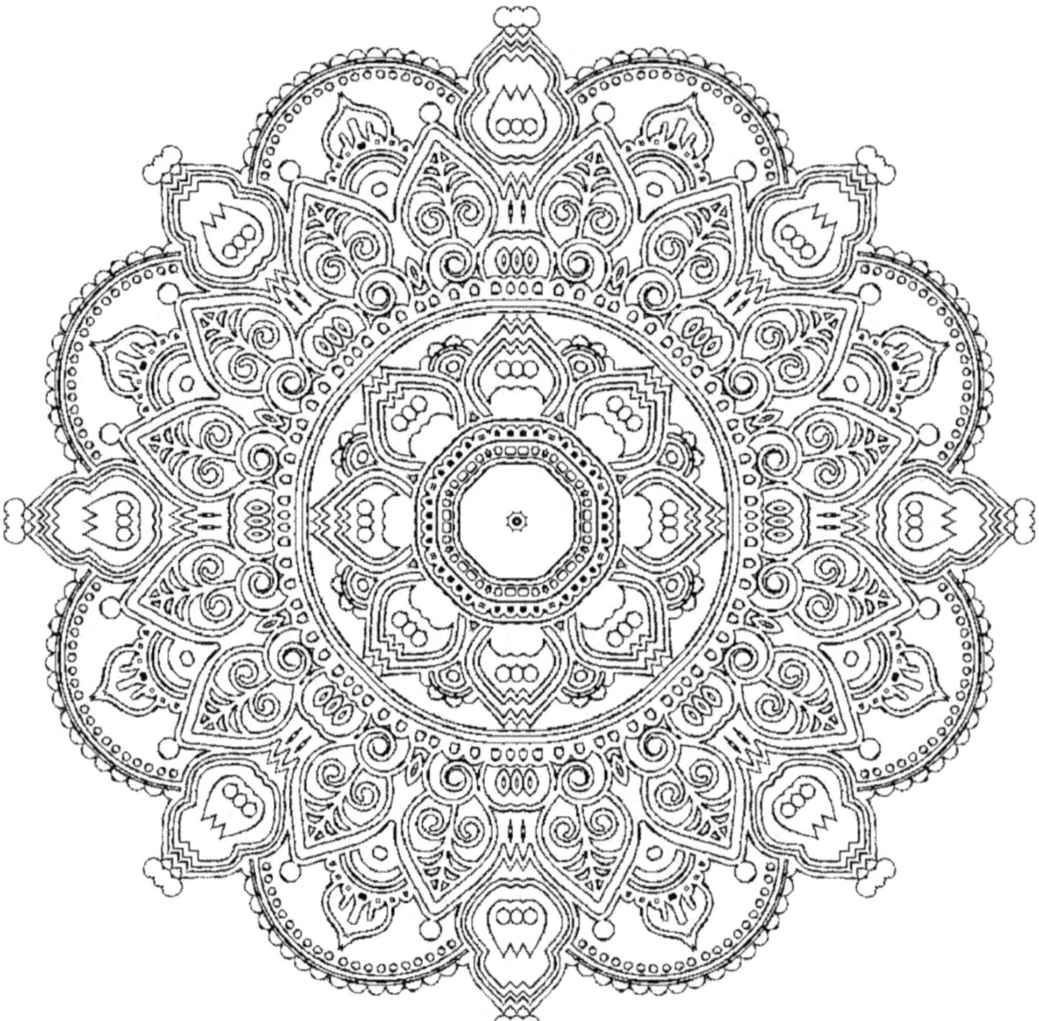

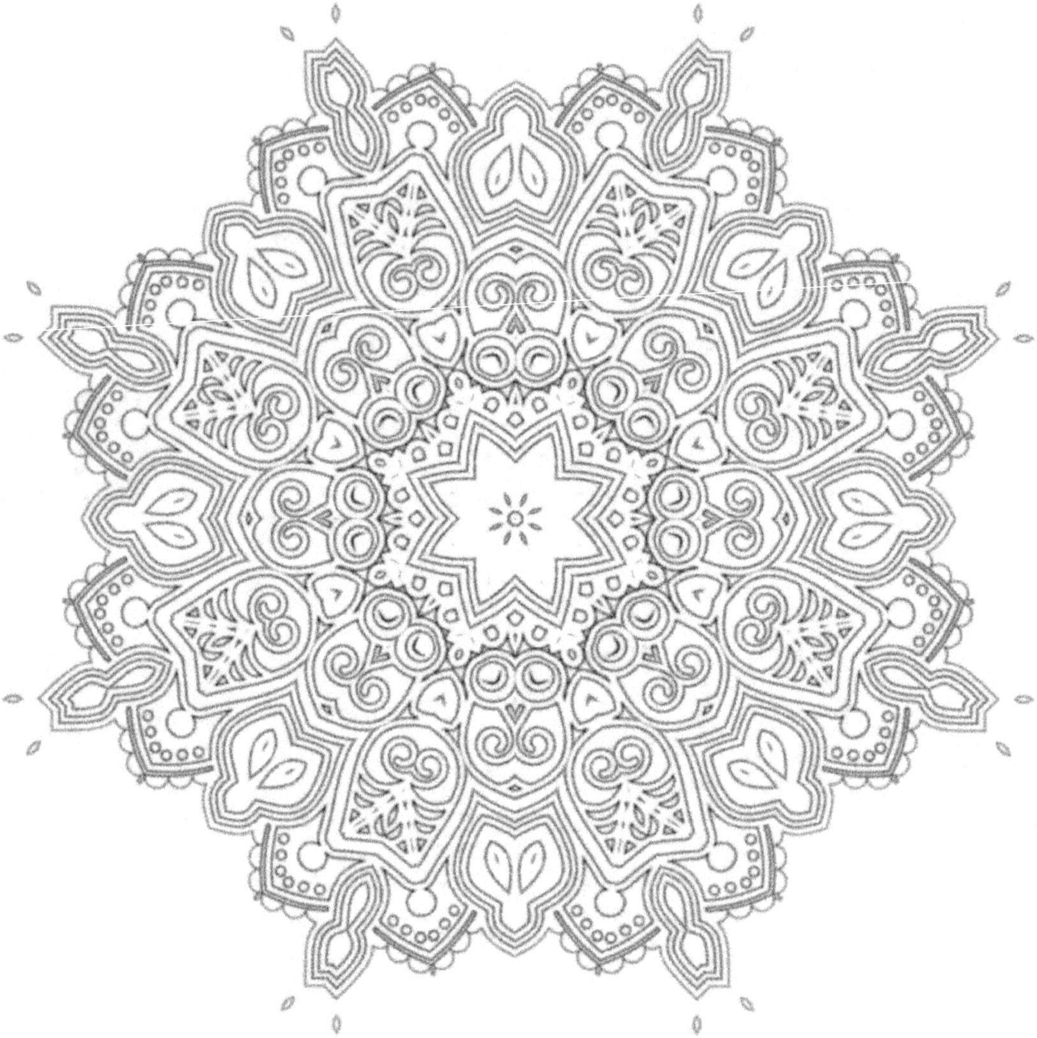

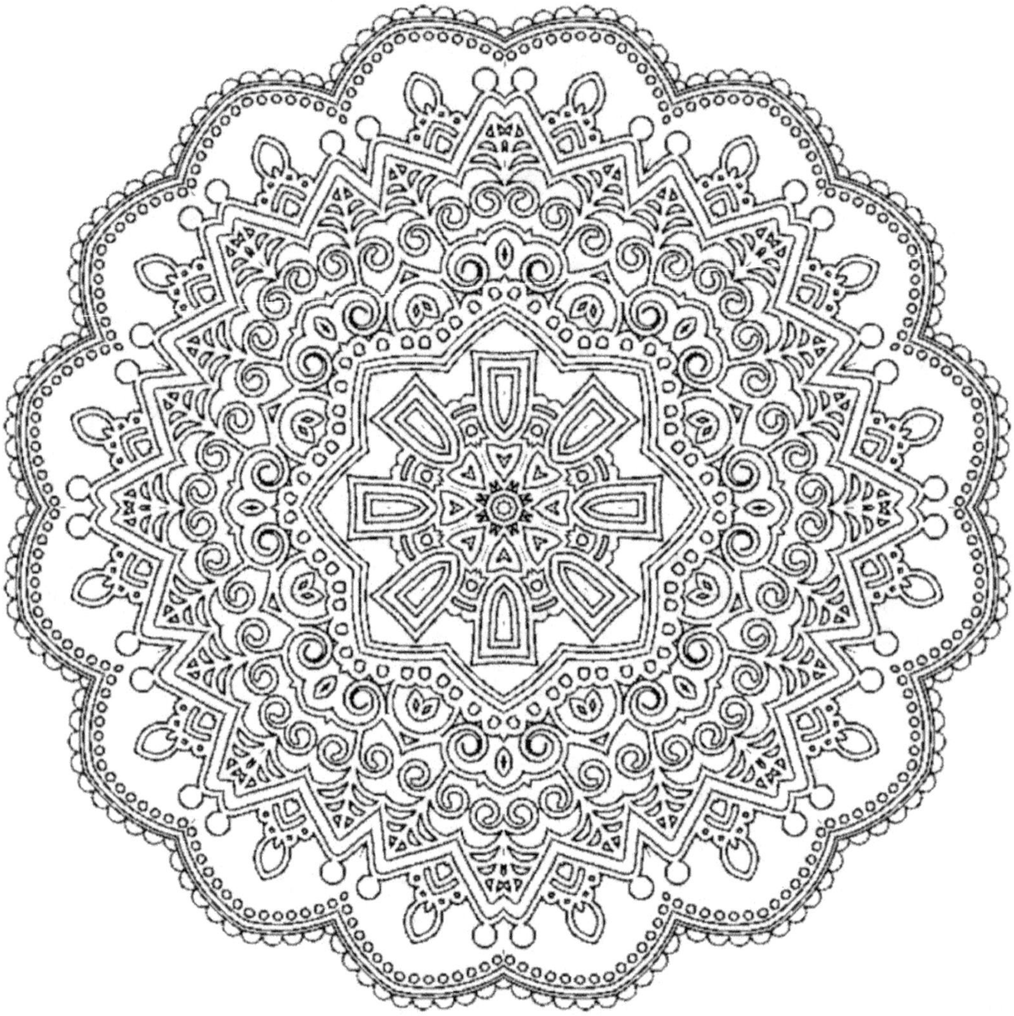

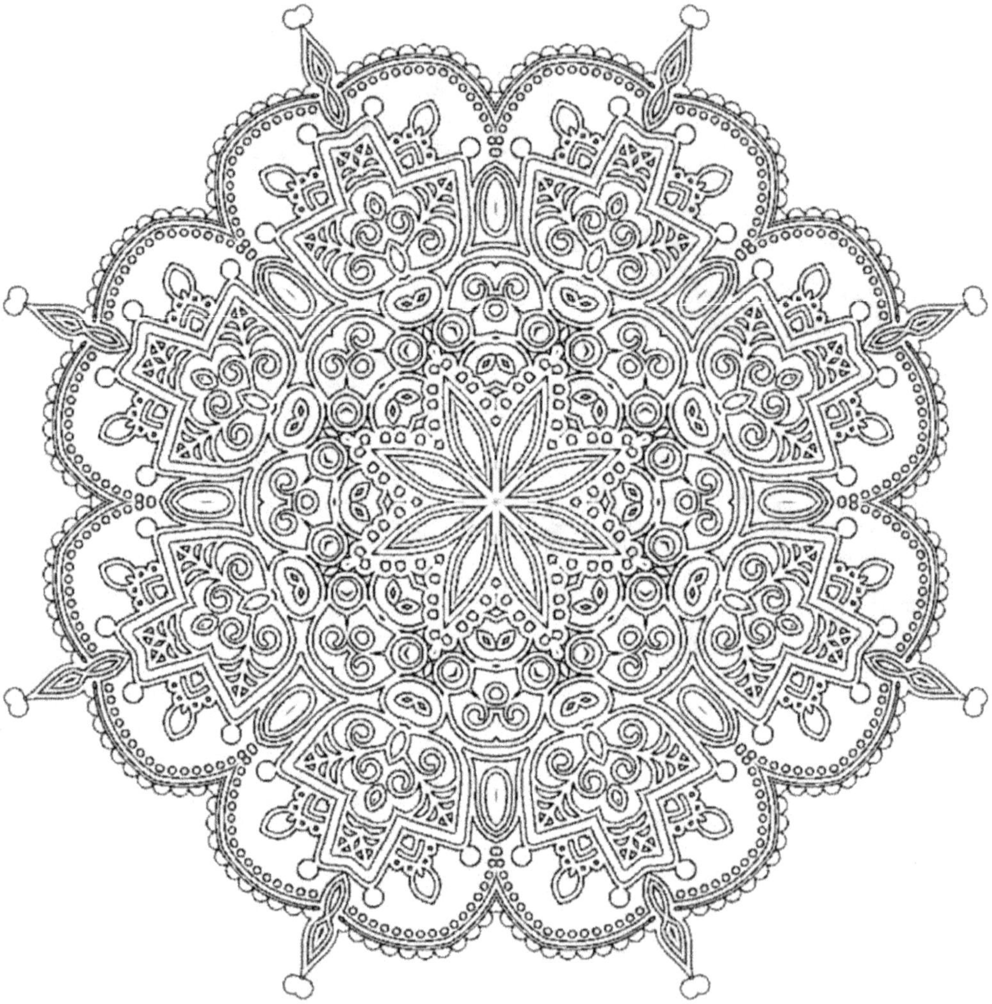

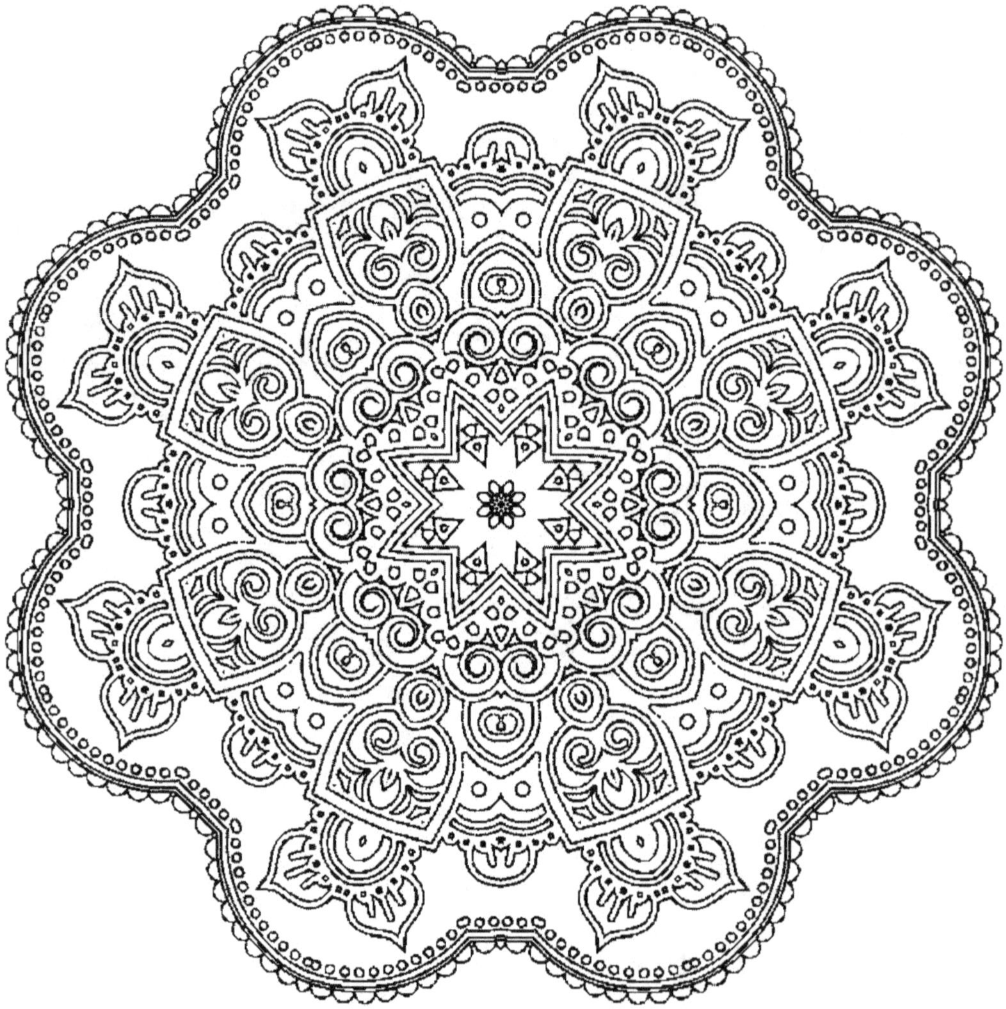

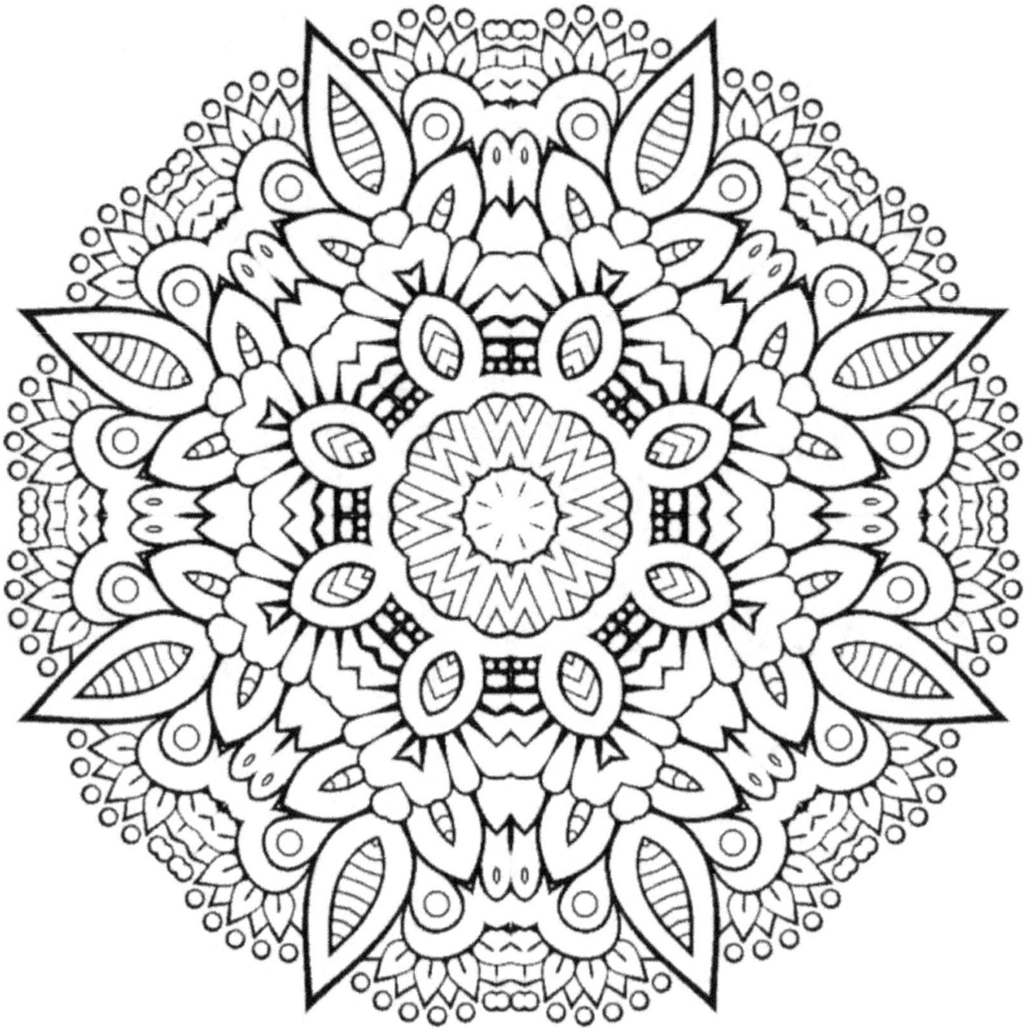

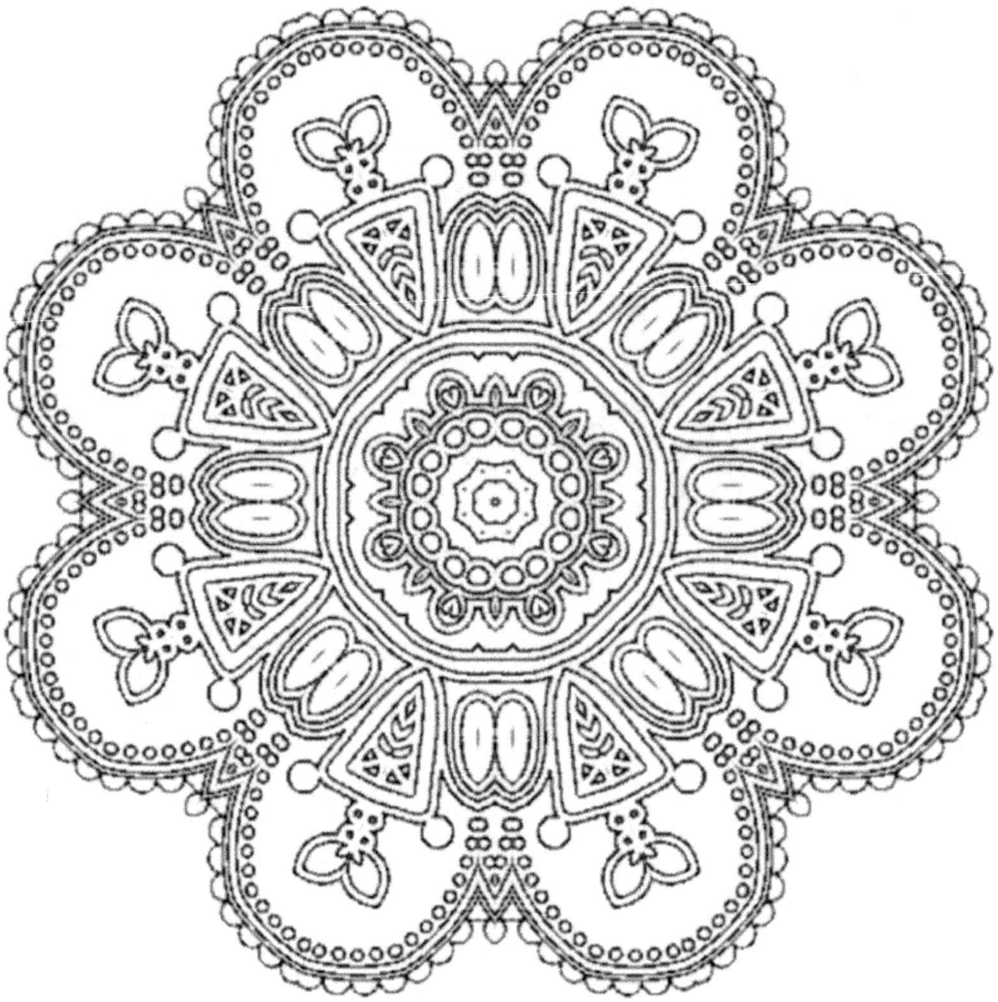

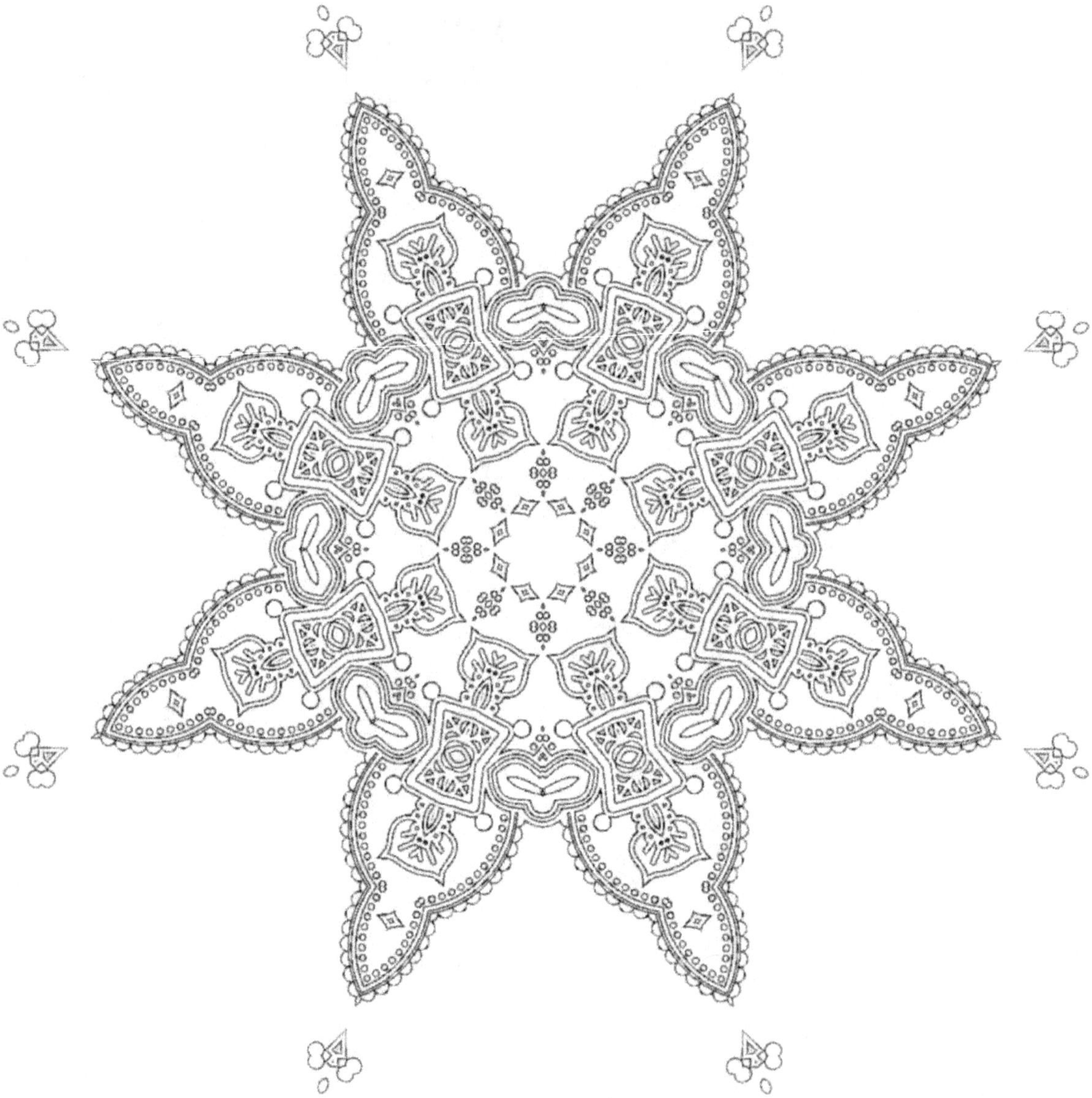

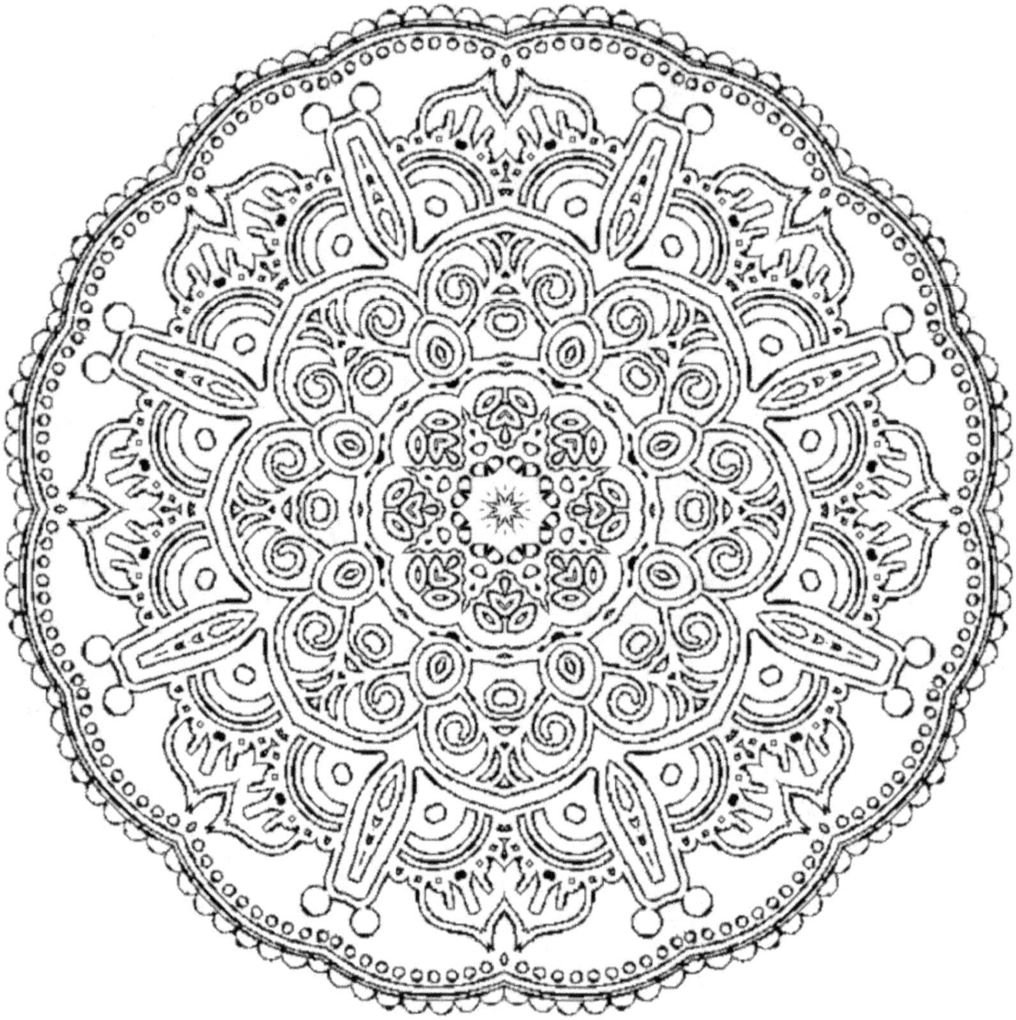

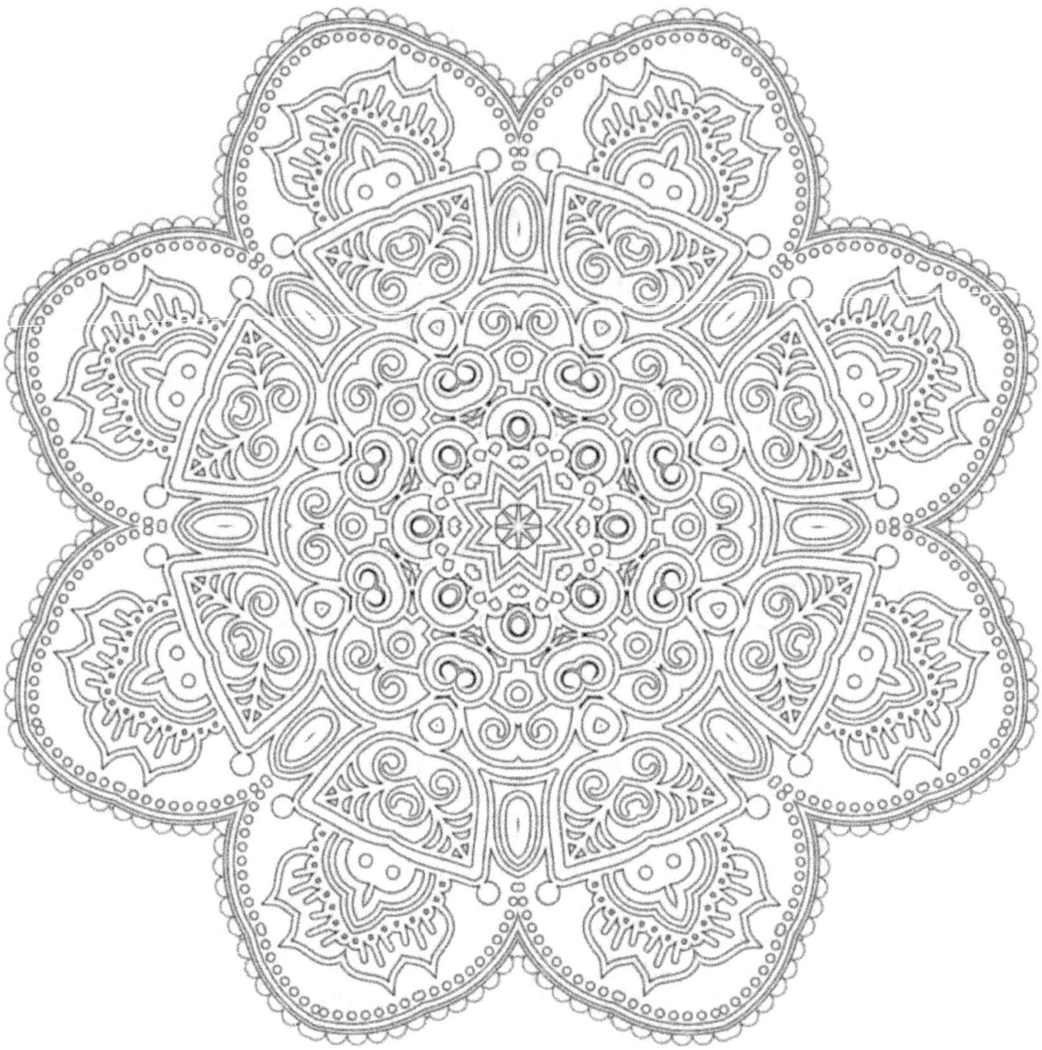

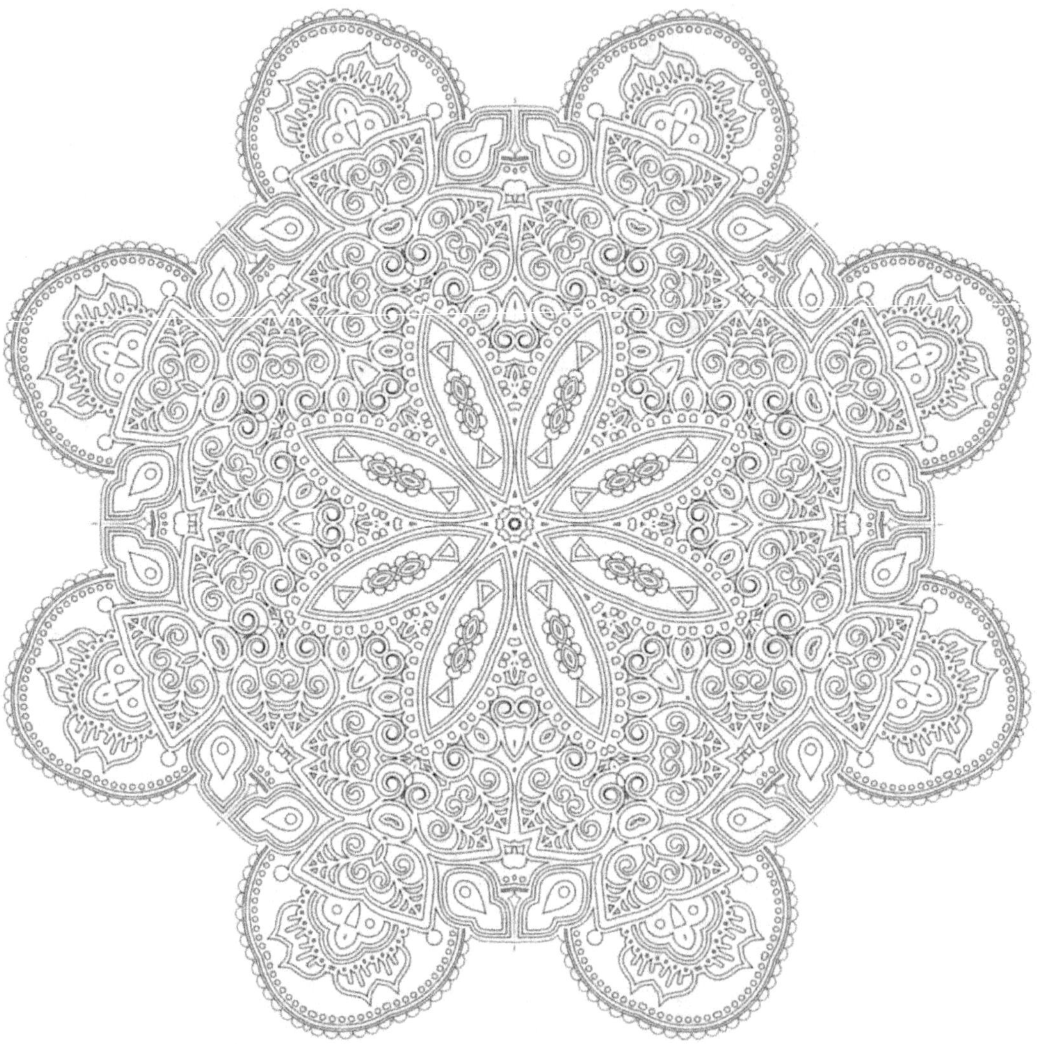

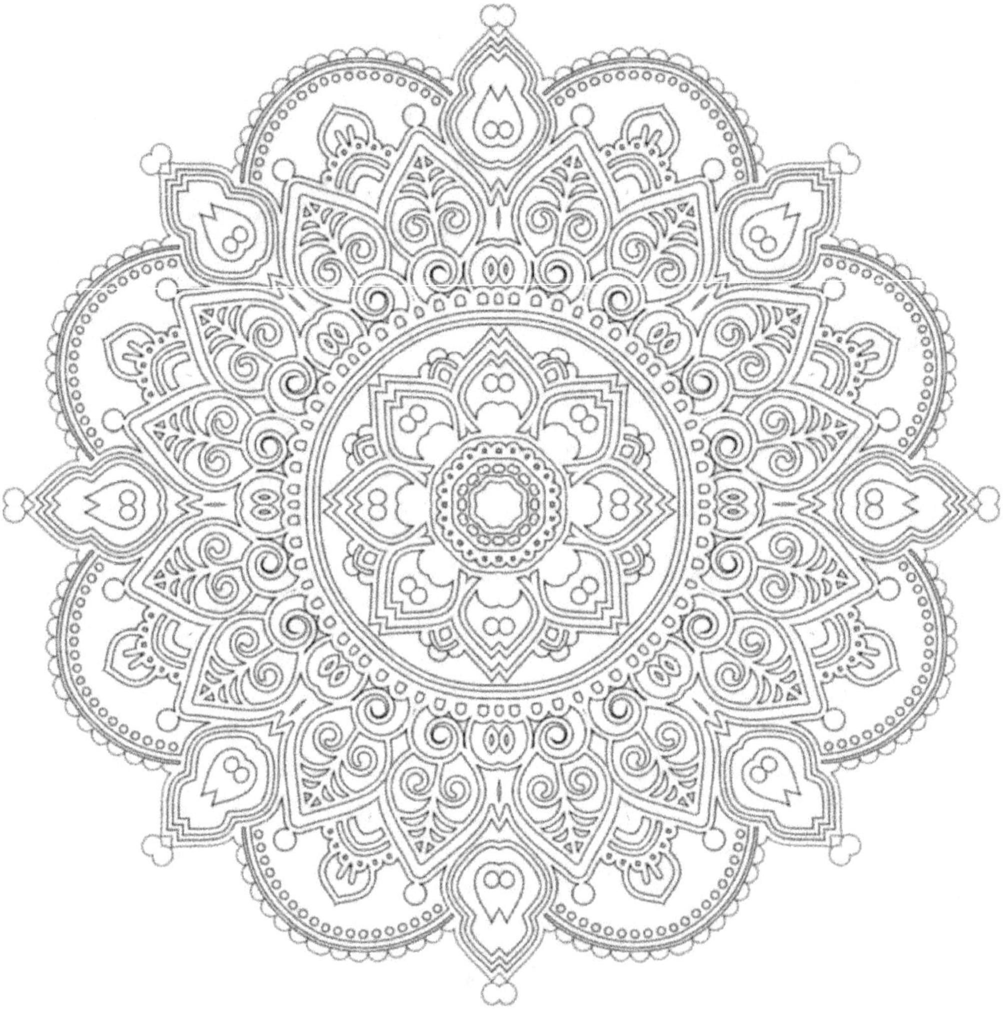

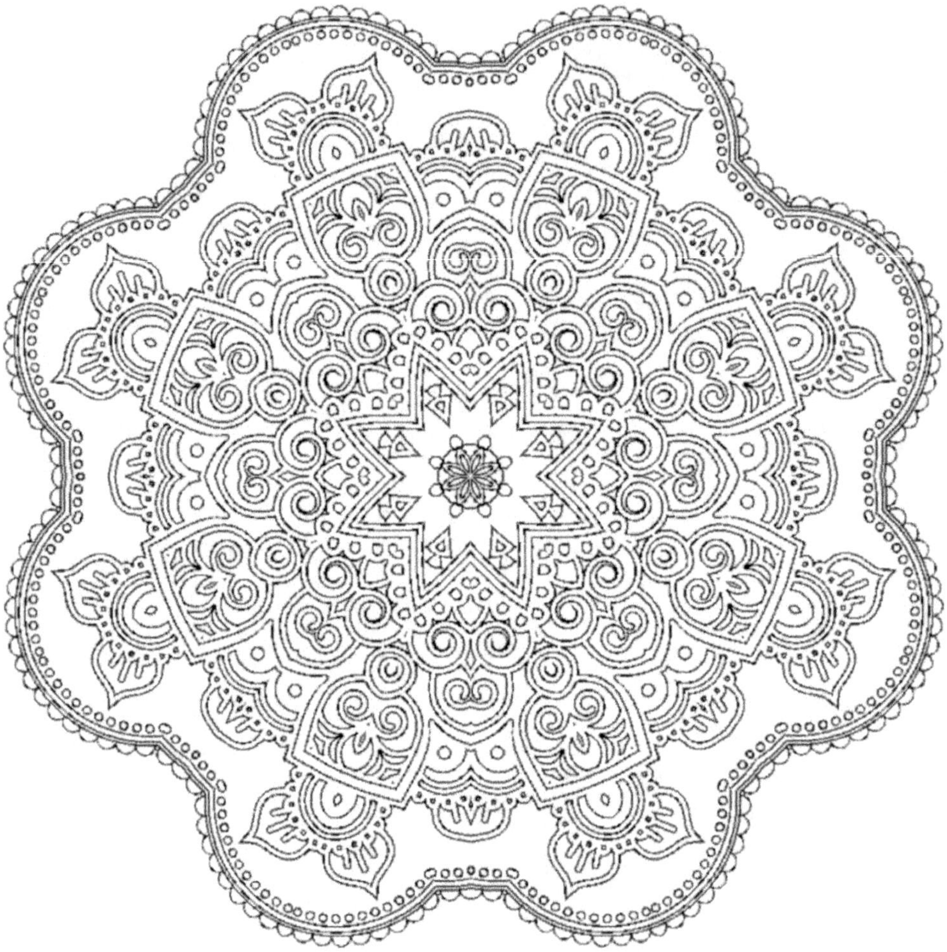

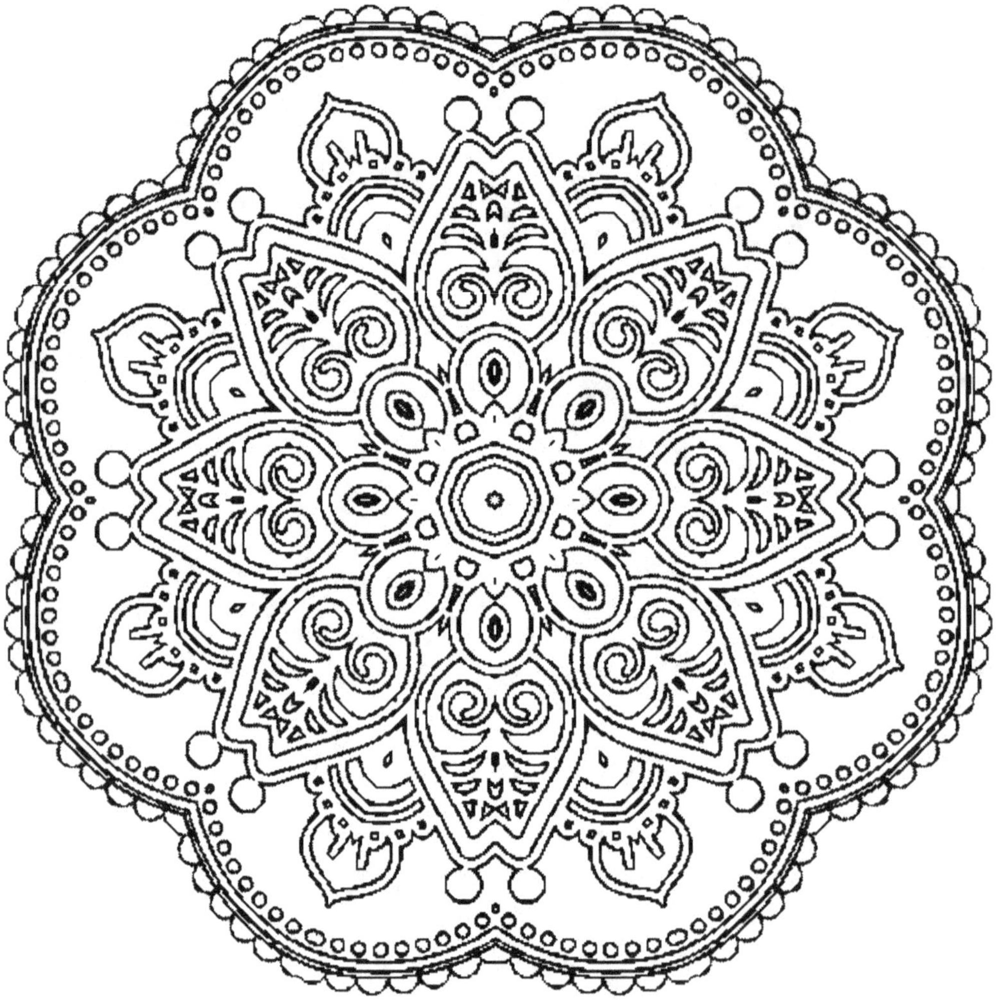

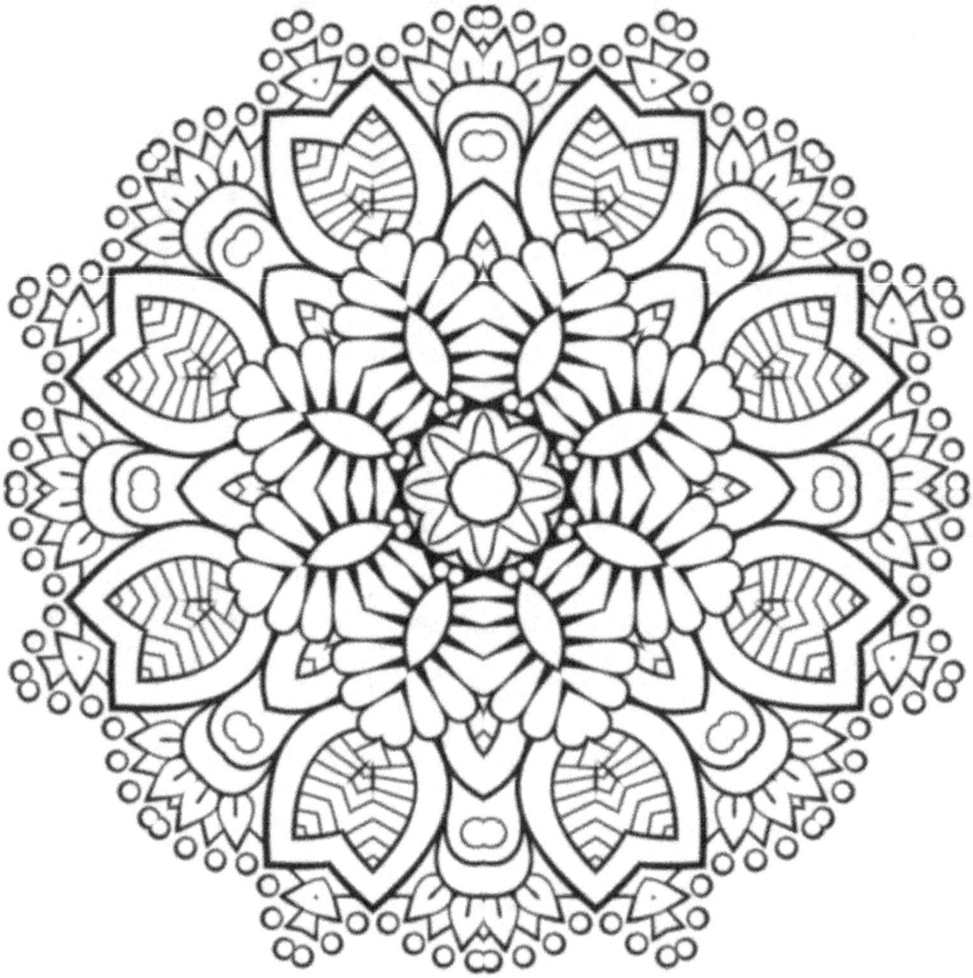

www.ingramcontent.com/pod-product-compliance
Lightning Source LLC
Chambersburg PA
CBHW080818220526
45466CB00011BB/3602
* 9 7 8 1 6 8 6 0 8 7 2 2 6 *